Beyond the Handlebars

Part 2

Robert and Evelyn Lee

Copyright© 2025 Robert and Evelyn Lee

ISBN: 978-1-62249-760-7

Published by
Biblio Publishing
Columbus, Ohio
BiblioPublishing.com

Table of Contents

Michigan – June 2019	1
Wisconsin – August 2019	3
Missouri – September 2019	6
South Dakota, Nebraska, Colorado – September 2020	8
Wyoming, Montana – September 2020	11
North Dakota, Minnesota – September 2020	15
Mississippi, Louisiana – October 2020	19
Georgia – February 2021	22
New Jersey, Delaware – May 2021	25
New Mexico – May 2021	27
Arizona – May 2021	29
Utah – May 2021	31
Kansas – May 2021	35
New York – July 2021	38
Connecticut, Rhode Island – September 2021	41
Massachusetts – September 2021	44
Maine, New Hampshire – September 2021	47

Robert and Evelyn Lee

Vermont – September 2021	50
Pennsylvania – October 2021	55
Virginia – November 2021	59
Iowa – December 2021	62
North Carolina – May 2022	66
Indiana, Ohio – August 2022	70
Alaska – September 2022	73
Idaho, Washington – September 2022	77
Oregon – September 2022	79
North Carolina, South Carolina – January 2023	81
Pennsylvania – August 2023	84
Nevada, California – September 2023	86
Hawaii – September 2023	90

We had already ridden on trails in 15 to 20 states before deciding to make it a goal to ride trails in all 50 states. That goal was reached on the island of Kauai, Hawaii, in September, 2023.

We rode our own bicycles in most states while choosing to rent in just five states: Alaska, The Pacific Northwest (Washington, Oregon, Idaho), and Hawaii. The bicycles we rented were all of a proper fit and comfortable.

As we reflect on all the trails we have ridden, we thoroughly enjoyed most of them. In many of the states, we have ridden multiple trails. And in some of the states, our rides were multi-day events, during which we secured hotels along the way. There were very few flat tires or bicycle repairs needed. We do remember the one day we endured two flat tires. Luckily, this day happened near a city with bicycle repair shops within a short distance.

Meeting lots of interesting people on the trails meant learning about the area in which we were riding. We could then visit the sites and attractions most beloved by the residents. On a lot of the trails, we also met other travelers not familiar with the area. That also meant for interesting conversations about the places of their residences. What a blessing it has been to complete this journey.

We wish to thank Evelyn's sister, Mary Lehman, for editing this second book.

The scripture quotations are from the King James Version unless otherwise noted.

Robert and Evelyn Lee

We continue to ride our bicycles most days as weather permits. The Kokosing Gap Trail in our hometown of Mount Vernon, Ohio, is our go-to trail. As our family has grown, we cherish each opportunity to spend as much time as possible with our children and their spouses (Karen and Jeremy, Tom and Sarah) and our grandchildren (Isaac, Audrey, Winnie, and Allie).

"Truth is powerful and it prevails".
Sojourner Truth

Michigan – Battle Creek is known across the globe as the breakfast cereal capital of the world.

June 2019

One of the highlights of riding the Battle Creek Linear Trail in Battle Creek, Michigan, was learning more about Sojourner Truth. She was a women's rights activist best known for her speech "Ain't I a Women?" on racial inequalities. Born into slavery, she escaped with her infant daughter to freedom in 1826. Born Isabella Baumfree in New York, she later changed her name to Sojourner Truth after having a spiritual calling, following God's urging to preach about abolitionism and equal rights for all. Battle Creek became her home and the Sojourner Truth Monument there is well done.

The trail through Battle Creek allowed us to trek to parks, monuments, and museums, all near the path. The trail was very well maintained. Home to the Kellogg brothers, who embraced health and wellness, Battle Creek has murals and a beautiful downtown, inspiring city leaders to create this wonderful trail. Along the way, there are gazebos, gardens, fountains and historical markers. We were able to sit in a downtown park and enjoy lunch while viewing artwork and a lovely cascading waterfall.

While tours of the Kellogg plant are no longer offered, as you traverse the trail you can see the historic Kellogg House. Kellogg has invested in downtown revitalization projects, which is evident as one rides the trail and observes the beauty of Battle Creek.

The cereal industry has been hurt for much of the past decade as cereal consumption has slowed nationally. However, Battle Creek is still the cereal city. Along with Kellogg's, Post's cereals roots are also in Battle Creek. The two companies have left their mark on the city, building both office buildings and local attractions. The Leila Arboretum was created by the widow of C W Post, founder of Post Cereals. The Arboretum is part of 7,000 acres of parkland in Battle Creek. The Battle Creek Regional History Museum is planned to open in the summer of 2020 and will display the wonderful history of this region of Michigan.

"Lead me in thy truth, and teach me."
Psalm 25:5

"The pessimist complains about the wind, the optimist expects it to change; the realist adjusts the sails."
William Arthur Ward, Writer

Wisconsin – Milwaukee, the largest city in Wisconsin, is a vibrant city on the western shore of Lake Michigan.

August 2019

Connecting the cities of Manitowoc and Two Rivers, Wisconsin, along Lake Michigan, the Mariners Trail is a beautiful hard-surfaced trail. A very pleasant cool lake breeze was present as we rode the length of the trail. Meticulously cared for gardens were planted along the way further enhancing the gorgeous shoreline scenery. In addition, beautiful artwork along this trail made for an even more interesting ride. One such art piece was titled "Wings of an Eagle". An eagle ready to soar from its high up nest had wings spread wide, and its front breast was lifted up like an airplane upon takeoff. What awesome metal artwork!

We rode from Two Rivers south to Manitowoc, where there is a submarine and also the Wisconsin Maritime Museum. We had not heard of Manitowoc prior to watching the Netflix Series "Making a Murderer", the story of Steven Avery. He served 18 years in prison for wrongful conviction of sexual assault and attempted murder, was released but later charged with murder and convicted of this crime which occurred two years after his release. The handling of the case was highly controversial, and the Netflix Series won several awards in exploring the criminal justice system.

Robert and Evelyn Lee

The Oak Leaf Trail in Milwaukee was also a good experience. This trail has over 125 miles of trail in and around the city of Milwaukee. We rode a portion of this trail beginning at the Milwaukee Art Museum. This museum is one of the largest in the United States, containing nearly 25,000 works of art. The building is an architectural landmark. The War Memorial part of the building is modern and shaped like a floating cross, with wings cantilevered from a central base. Time magazine called it "one of the country's finest examples of modern architecture put to work for civic purposes". An addition to the building features a cathedral-like space with a vaulted glass ceiling, a moveable sunscreen with a 217-foot wingspan that unfolds and folds twice daily, and a pedestrian suspension bridge that connects the Museum to the city.

We enjoyed the Oak Leaf Trail, with most of the part we rode being along Lake Michigan. Many sailboats were out and the breeze from the lake made for an enjoyable ride on this very warm summer day. The trail was busy along the Lake Loop.

"He answered and said unto them, When it is evening ye say, it will be fair weather: for the sky is red. And in the morning, it will be foul weather today: for the sky is red and lowering. O ye hypocrites, ye can discern the face of the sky; but can you not discern the signs of the times?"
                                        Matthew 16:2,3

Beyond the Handlebars Part 2

> "In every walk with nature, one receives far more than he seeks."
> John Muir, Father of the National Parks

Missouri – The Katy Trail is the country's longest recreational rail trail.

September 2019

For two beautiful days in September 2019, we rode parts of the Katy Trail. The trail is approximately 240 miles and runs across Missouri from Clinton in the west to St. Charles near St. Louis in the east. More than half the trail follows Lewis and Clark's path up the Missouri River.

While on the portion of the trail along the Missouri River, you ride beneath towering sandstone river bluffs on one side and the Missouri River on the other. Eagles circle overhead. Maya Angelou, a native of Missouri, once said "Life is not measured by the number of breaths you take but by the moments that take your breath away." It seems she must surely have visited this part of her home state!

In May 1804, Meriwether Lewis and William Clark led an expedition up the Missouri River and would not return until September 1806. They made many stops along the river where now the Katy Trail exists. These stops are mentioned in their journal writings. In May, they passed by the Daniel Boone settlement near today's Marthesville. In June, they traveled through the scenic bluff country, passing Roche Percee Natural Arch. Clark recorded the pictographs he saw painted on the bluff that the Katy Trail tunnel now passes through near Rocheport. In the course of their journey, Lewis

Beyond the Handlebars Part 2

and Clark acquired knowledge of numerous tribes of Indians previously unknown, they became informed about the trade they could carry on with them, and they were enabled to give accuracy of the geography. Their expedition opened the door to further exploration, trade and scientific discoveries.

During the two days we were bicycling on this trail, the Woman Tour was out bicycling the trail as well. They just happened to be on the sections we rode. We chatted with some of the women, who told us they were doing the trail in its entirety in eight straight days of riding. Woman Tours is a fully-supported inn-to-inn road bike trips for women of all ages and abilities. They had a vehicle to carry luggage, provide meals, and shuttle women to hotels as they finish each day's ride. The women seemed to enjoy and said it didn't matter how slow or fast you rode, as long as you got the day's ride in by dark. Usually, they rode around 30 miles per day. Women Tours schedules bicycle trips for women both domestically and internationally.

We would like to ride the rest of the Katy Trail sometime. It takes a little longer because it is not paved. It had rained quite a bit the days before we rode, so it was a bit more difficult; however it was very doable. With nature's beauty all along the way, we understand why many bicyclists proclaim this their favorite trail.

"But ask now the beasts, and they shall teach thee; and the fowls of the air, and they shall tell thee: Or speak to the earth, and it shall teach thee; and the fishes of the sea shall declare unto thee. Who knoweth not in all these that the hand of the Lord hath wrought this? In whose hand is the soul of every living thing, and the breath of all mankind."
Job 12:7-10

"As I've learned in my time in the state legislature, important legislation is always a work in progress."
Marco Rubio

South Dakota — Famous for landmarks such as Mount Rushmore, Badlands, and Crazy Horse Memorial. South Dakota is the only state whose name shares no letters with its capital.

Nebraska — Atop the 400 foot tower of the Nebraska State Capitol stands "The Sower", representing Nebraska's agricultural heritage.

Colorado — The 13th step of the state capitol building in Denver is exactly one mile high above sea level.

September 2020

Along the small Dakota Dunes Trail in South Dakota, one will see Iowa on the other side of the Big Sioux River and Nebraska on the other side of the Missouri River. The very

Beyond the Handlebars Part 2

well maintained trail in the southeastern corner of South Dakota runs through flat and open fields that border Interstate 29 and then the Big Sioux River before heading to the confluence of the Big Sioux and the Missouri Rivers and the place where the borders of Iowa, South Dakota, and Nebraska all meet. Although a short trail, it was well worth riding.

The Johnson Lake Hike and Bike Trail around a popular recreational lake in Nebraska was a delight. Most of the trail is paved and traverses around the shoreline. A few sections proceed along well-marked shared roadways. This delightful trail was a very enjoyable break on our trip to several states where we had previously not ridden our bicycles. Johnson Lake was beautiful. The nearly 11 miles we rode around this lake was peaceful, with little traffic, and gorgeous views of the lake. The area also featured large, mature trees which helped keep the sun at bay.

After this pleasant biking experience, we drove on to Colorado to bicycle the Bear Creek Trail connecting downtown Denver with the foothills of the Rockies. The trail was relatively flat and very nice. There were scenic views of the woodlands, meadows, and Bear Creek. And at times, the Denver skyline was in view.

On this trip with the coronavirus pandemic still ongoing, we fixed up our vehicle so we could camp out and not use hotels. This worked out very well. It was very comfortable and the weather was perfect. As we made our way through Nebraska and into Colorado, we drove past the State Capitol Buildings in these states. First, on our way to Johnson Lake from the corner of three states (Iowa, South Dakota, and Nebraska), we passed through several Indian reservations, and then drove through Lincoln. We drove past the Capitol Building. The Nebraska State Capitol has an office tower. Clad with Indiana limestone, the Capitol has a low wide base in a "cross within a square", creating four interior courtyards. This base is three levels in height. From the center rises a 400 foot domed tower. On top of this tower is a 19 foot tall bronze figure of "The Sower". As we passed by, we realized how impressive this building looked. A protest on the front steps was in progress, with a Native American in full headdress speaking. Because this was during the pandemic, we decided to be safe and just drive by rather than park and get out of the vehicle. We took several photos and continued on our journey toward Johnson Lake.

The following day, as we went into Denver, we again drove by the Capitol Building. This building was designed on an axis in the form of a Greek cross and resembles the basic design of the nation's Capitol in Washington, D.C. It was also an impressive building. Again, because it was a busy area, we chose to simply drive by while snapping a few photos.

On this trip, we would continue on through Wyoming, Montana, North Dakota, Minnesota, and Wisconsin (where we stopped to spend a few days with our son, daughter-in-law, and granddaughter) before returning to our home in Ohio.

"Love worketh no ill to his neighbor: therefore love is the fulfilling of the law."
Romans 13:10

"You're off to great places! Today is your day! Your mountain is waiting, so. . . . get on *your way!*"

Dr. *Seuss*

Wyoming – Wyoming territory became first in the nation to grant women the right to vote in 1869. Also, the first female governor in the country was elected in Wyoming.

Montana – Montana is the largest landlocked state in the United States.

September 2020

 Casper, Wyoming, nicknamed "The Oil City", is the second largest city in Wyoming, with Cheyenne, the state capital, being the largest. Casper has a history of oil boomtown and cowboy culture. Ranked high on the list of best cities to raise a family, Casper has a vibrant arts community, is a regional center of banking and commerce, and is home to a number of museums and historical sites.
 While in Casper, we rode The Platte River Trail and also spent a few hours climbing Casper Mountain from Rotary Park and Garden Creek Falls.

Robert and Evelyn Lee

We began our bicycling of the Platte River Trail at the North Casper Sports Complex. The trail mostly follows the river. At the time we were there, some parts of the 10 mile trail were being repaired. At a few points, we had to walk our bicycles around some construction. But the rest of the trail was in excellent condition.

The hike on Casper Mountain was marvelous. We chose to do this hike in the early morning so as not to pass many hikers; hoping to not wear masks as much (coronavirus pandemic was still a problem, requiring mask wearing if you could not distance). This worked really well. The entire hike found us only passing one other hiker. Beginning at Rotary Park at the base of Casper Mountain, the trail proved to be well-maintained. Garden Creek Falls is one of Casper's most treasured spots. We saw the falls from various places as we climbed. When up on this picturesque mountain sitting among the trees, it's easy to forget you are just a few miles from the city. On the climb, we passed scenic overlooks, magnificent photo opportunities and "lookout" platforms. Though steep, the trails to these platforms had steel ropes to help negotiate the rocks to get to the platforms. We were really happy with the decision to hike very early as, when we were finishing our hike, many people were beginning to arrive at the base of the mountain to begin their own hikes.

We were happy to have spent a few days in Casper. It is a beautiful place and a destination well worth visiting. The trip reminded me of a saying I have heard on different occasions. I believe the author is unknown – "Memories made in the mountains stay in our hearts forever".

The following day we rode Swords Park Trail in Billings, Montana. The trail was uphill for quite a ways along the sandstone formation known as Rimrocks. Once up the initial hill, the view is very scenic overlooking Billings. If you want flat, this trail is not for you. Near the beginning of the trail, we visited Boothill Cemetery, which sits near "The Place Where the White Horse Went Down". Boothill Cemetery, on a hill in Billings, was so named because so many occupants went to their deaths with their boots on. Most famous buried there was H. M. Taylor, scout who took news of Custer Massacre of 1876 from the battle area to Bozeman. Most others buried there died from disease, gunfights, accidents and suicides.

In 1837-38 the terrible disease of smallpox affected all Montana Indian tribes. They had no immunity. Two young warriors returning from a war expedition found their village stricken. Both of them found friends and family dead and dying and were despondent. They dressed in their finest clothing, mounted a snow-white horse and drove the blindfolded horse over a cliff. Time has reduced the height of the cliff, but the location is remembered to this day as "The Place Where the White Horse Went Down".

"For ye shall go out with joy, and be led forth with peace; the mountains and the hills shall break forth before you into singing, and all the trees of the field shall clap their hands."
Isaiah 55:12

Robert and Evelyn Lee

"The Mississippi River will always have its own way; no engineering skill can persuade it to do otherwise."
Mark Twain

North Dakota – Salem Sue is one of the most popular of North Dakota's roadside sculptures.

Minnesota – The Mississippi River begins as a small knee-deep river flowing out of Lake Itasca in northwestern Minnesota.

September 2020

 Driving through the state of North Dakota west to east seemed long as we were on the same road the entire way through. Driving on Route 94, we stopped several times to break up the ride. One such stop was to walk up the hill to see Salem Sue in New Salem. Salem Sue is a giant fiberglass Holstein cow sculpture built in 1974 in honor of the local dairy farming industry. The statue stands 38 feet high and 50 feet long. It was a fun place to get out of the car and stretch the legs a bit.

 A goal of ours was to visit the place where the Mississippi River begins. We drove toward Bemidji in Northwestern Minnesota where we planned to stay the night. As it turned out, Lake Itasca was very near there and we saw signs for visitors to the area with directions to the headwaters of the

Robert and Evelyn Lee

Mississippi. Since a few hours of daylight remained, we followed directions and were not disappointed. There were other visitors there, and since we had an hour left before closing, we went and stuck our toes in the waters that marked the start of the Mississippi, took photos, and enjoyed this short visit.

The following day, we rode some trails on our way to Janesville, WI. We were excited to visit our son, daughter-in-law, and granddaughter for a few days before heading home to Ohio.

"He that believeth on me, as the scriptures hath said, out of his belly shall flow rivers of living water."
John 7:38

Beyond the Handlebars Part 2

> "I've always loved magnolia trees and their blooms – there's something so beautiful about a magnolia blossom. It demands attention, and you can't help but love those big, creamy petals and that fragrant smell."
> Joanna Gaines, The Magnolia Story

Mississippi – Blues music was born in the Mississippi Delta, the northwest section of the state between the Mississippi and Yazoo Rivers.

Louisiana – the only state in the country with "parishes" instead of counties.

October 2020

    The state flower of both Mississippi and Louisiana is the magnolia. This flowering plant symbolizes longevity and perseverance and can also represent nobility, love for nature, and beauty. While the magnolias were not in bloom when we visited these two states to bicycle, the cotton fields were many, wide, and pleasing to the eye. These fields appeared as if an expanse of snow had fallen. But it wasn't the look of a heavy snow; instead the white appeared light and airy.

    While in Mississippi, we rode our bicycles on the Tanglefoot Trail, Mississippi's longest Rails to Trails conversion meandering 43.6 miles through the foothills of the Appalachian Mountains. The asphalt path connects six communities – New Albany, Ecru, Pontotoc, Algoma, New Houlka, and Houston. We rode the approximately 23 miles roundtrip between New Albany and Ecru. It was scenic, well-maintained, and relatively flat. The slight change in elevation made our choice of beginning in New Albany wise since the slight downhill would come during the return from Ecru. If we had more time, we would have liked to ride the rest of the trail. The part we did was a wonderful experience. The trail supporters were recognized on markers along the way. We loved this nice touch. New Albany was delightful. There were small cafes and quaint shops if one wanted to shop or catch a bite to eat. The courthouse there was beautiful.

From Mississippi, we drove on to Slidell, Louisiana, to ride the Tammany Trace, a rail trail occupying a former Illinois Central Railroad corridor. This was a nice easy, flat surface. The trail is well kept and has beautiful pine forest scenery. We did encounter a rather large pine snake, a nonvenomous species endemic to the southeastern United States. It was along the right side of the trail, was rather large, coiled, and not moving. We passed by without any trouble and did not see it on the return ride. The weather was warmer than usual for a mid-October day in the south.

Slidell begins where Lake Pontchartrain ends, where the lake forges towards the Gulf of Mexico. The marshlands provide an industry of swamp tours where one can see the lush growth of the Louisiana swamp. Along with cypress trees and abundant flora, one may see alligators, snakes, turtles, birds and other wildlife.

The New Orleans cemetery tours are very educational. The cemeteries are referred to as "Cities of the Dead". The loved ones in New Orleans are interred above ground. The water table is very high. The early settlers could not keep the caskets from literally floating. The water table would pop the

Beyond the Handlebars Part 2

coffins out of the ground. The early settlers tried placing stones in and on top of the coffins. This didn't work. Then they tried boring holes in the coffins. This also proved unsuitable. Eventually, graves were kept above ground, using vaults.

We enjoyed this trip south to ride in two states in which we had not previously ridden. The drive home was very pleasant and relaxing. The beauty of the trees in the fall season, especially with the sun shining on them, was outstanding.

"He has made everything beautiful in its time. He has also set eternity in the human heart; yet no one can fathom what God has done from beginning to end."

Ecclesiastes 3:11 New International Version

"Do all the good you can, By all the means you can, In all the ways you can, In all the places you can, At all the times you can, To all the people you can, As long as ever you can."
John Wesley

Georgia – The Golden Isles of Georgia on the coast on the Atlantic Ocean are comprised of the city of Brunswick and four barrier islands (St. Simons Island, Sea Island, Jekyll Island, and Little St. Simons Island).

February 2021

On this trip to Georgia, we visited St. Simons Island and Jekyll Island. We had been to these islands in 2005 and again in 2011. This trip we visited Fort Frederica on St. Simons. This fort was established in 1736 by James Oglethorpe to protect the southern boundary of his new colony of Georgia from the Spanish in Florida. We walked along the path where this military outpost and town had been and viewed the many archeological dig findings from the area. The Battle of "Bloody Marsh" was fought here and Oglethorpe convinced the Spanish to retreat from Georgia seven days later. The British victory confirmed Georgia was British territory, peace was declared, and Frederica's Regiment was disbanded.

A very short distance from Fort Frederica, we stood near the place where John Wesley preached under a large oak tree. Another large oak (approximately 250 years old) near the one he preached under commemorated the spot.

Beyond the Handlebars Part 2

We rode our bicycles on this island and found many good bicycle paths to traverse. On several other occasions in prior years, we had ridden the path past the airport on Frederica Road to Kings Way and then followed Kings Way to the downtown and to the pier. Located on the south end of the island, Pier Village was very popular for gathering, dining and shopping. The pier on the ocean allows views of the lighthouse and Jekyll Island. Going north on the bicycle trail, you can bicycle along Frederica Road to Cannon Point Preserve to view wildlife, and back to the path which goes on to Fort Frederica.

On Jekyll Island, we were pleasantly surprised at how many new bicycle paths had been constructed. In prior years, we had ridden much of the twenty miles around the perimeter of the island on the roads. But in 2021 on this trip, we rode the island all on bicycle paths. We were able to ride to the historic district, as well as past the Georgia Sea Turtle Center and to Driftwood Beach, as the trail circled the island.

We had previously visited the Sea Turtle Center, even witnessing a surgery on a large turtle. So on this trip, we did not visit the Center again, but we had fond memories of learning about the turtles in 2011. We did stop and walk on Driftwood Beach, a very pretty area of Jekyll Island. From Driftwood Beach, you could see the crews erecting barriers around the cargo ship that had capsized in the ocean off St. Simons Island in September of 2019. The plan is to cut the ship up once the environmental safety barriers are in place. They are hoping to have this ship totally removed prior to hurricane season in 2021.

Seeing the Grand Hotel in the historic district and dining on the Veranda of this beautiful resort was pleasant on this unusually warm day in late February on Jekyll Island.

Robert and Evelyn Lee

"Sing unto the Lord a new song, and His praise from the end of the earth, ye that go down to the sea, and all that is therein; the isles, and the inhabitants thereof."

Isaiah 42:10

"The peregrine falcon is much more than a fast bird; it's a symbol of resilience and survival."
Author Unknown

New Jersey — The Garden State, New Jersey's motto is "Liberty and Prosperity".

Delaware — The First State, Delaware's motto is "Liberty and Independence".

May 2021

    The Monroe Township Bike Path in Gloucester County, New Jersey runs between the towns of Glassboro and Williamstown. The hardwood-forested area was very pleasant as the ample tree cover made for shady trail travel. And the trail was wide, flat, and well paved.
    Williamstown and Glassboro were one-time glass manufacturing centers. The borough of Glassboro's name reflects the 19th century industry that thrived in this area. The trail follows the railroads that were originally conceived to serve the many glass and bottle makers in the area.
    The 12.4 mile Michael N. Castle C & D Canal Trail begins at the Delaware City Marina in Delaware City, Delaware, and ends at the Ben Cardin C & D Canal Recreational Trail at the Delaware/Maryland state line. Here, the trail becomes the Ben Cardin Trail, which runs for 1.8 miles to the historical, quaint canal town of Chesapeake City, Maryland. The ride on

these trails was just beautiful. There were plenty of benches on which to sit and watch the large ships in the canal.

The trail also features nature's beauty in its wildflowers, trees, and wildlife. There are plenty of rarer species of birds, such as peregrine falcons, grebes, and eagles. The peregrine falcon became an endangered species in many areas because of the widespread use of certain pesticides, especially DDT. Since the ban on DDT since the early 1970's, populations have recovered.

The combined C & D canal trails were named for Michael N. Castle, former governor and U.S. representative from Delaware, and Ben Cardin, senator from Maryland.

"O Lord, how manifold are your works! In wisdom you have made them all; the earth is full of your creatures."
Psalm 104:24   English Standard Version

"To walk in nature is to witness a thousand miracles."
Mary Davis

New Mexico – The northwest corner touches Arizona, Utah, and Colorado, creating the only spot where four states meet.

May 2021

We were pleasantly surprised at how much we enjoyed the Paseo del Bosque Trail in Albuquerque, New Mexico. Not only was the trail well maintained, the ride there proved to be a learning experience about bosques.

The trail goes along the Rio Grande for 16 miles. There are no intersections to worry about as bridges were built to pass over the trail, so the ride goes very well on this pretty much flat trail, with the only downs and ups being when passing under the bridges.

As we rode the trail, the cottonwood bosque was on both sides, and on one side beyond the bosque was the Rio Grande River. The word bosque is Spanish for woods. Bosques are an ecosystem found almost exclusively in the arid Southwest, mostly along the Rio Grande. The river, flowing through the center of the bosque, sustains this forested oasis.

The Paseo del Bosque Trail was a very scenic path through the bosque. Rio Grande cottonwoods have been growing in the bosque for more than a million years and are dependent on a reliable water supply for germination and survival. The cottonwoods reproduce by seeding; their seeds carried by downy white tufts dispersed by wind and water. The seedlings need bare soil, moisture and plenty of sunshine to germinate. The cottonwoods provide the canopy that allows lots of different types of animals and birds to live in the desert – porcupines, eagles, songbirds, Cooper's hawks, Red-tailed hawks, insects, spiders, rock squirrels, beavers and more.

Another highlight of our visit to Albuquerque was going to the Sandia Mountains and walking some of the trails. It was disappointing the Tramway was not running on Tuesday, but our walks were wonderful. Many different species of cacti were seen, some of them blooming. The Sandia Mountains appear a very pretty color of pink at sunset.

"But blessed is the one who trusts in the Lord, whose confidence is in him. They will be like a tree planted by the water that sends out its roots by the stream. It does not fear when heat comes; its leaves are always green. It has no worries in a year of drought and never fails to bear fruit."
Jeremiah 17:7-8   New International Version

"Baseball, it is said, is only a game. True. And the Grand Canyon is only a hole in Arizona. Not all holes, or games, are created equal."

George Will

Arizona – The Sonoran Desert is the only place on earth where the iconic saguaro cactus grows.

May 2021

Before riding the Grand Canyon Rim Trail, we decided to ride one other trail in Arizona. The Central Arizona Project Trail through the north side of Scottsdale is a fully paved trail which avoids busy roads by underpasses. The trail also has shade. This proved a real blessing as the temperature rose to 99 degrees the day we rode in late May. We started out when the temperature was 90 degrees and finished at 94 degrees. But the shade helped, and it did not seem that hot.

The path was gorgeous with beautiful flowers and cacti in full bloom. The trail was flat and scenic as it passed through park-like settings with lots of greenery and trees.

At the Grand Canyon the following day, we chose to ride from just past the Visitor's Center to Hermit's Rest. The road is closed to vehicle traffic, except for shuttle buses, from March 1 to November 30. As we rode along the South Rim, we stopped at most of the overlook points to view the spectacular Grand Canyon. Maricopa Point, Hopi Point, Mohave Point, The Abyss, Pima Point – all had wonderful vantage points to take in the beauty with which we were surrounded. When we reached our destination at Hermit's Rest, the western end of paved road along the South Rim, we found restrooms, picnic tables, and a refreshment stand. The ride was pleasant, sometimes uphill, but very doable. Some of the ride was on the very lightly traveled shuttle bus only roads and some on paved bicycle paths.

The Grand Canyon is a mile deep, 277 miles long and 18 miles wide. The Canyon was carved over some six million years, although no one is sure about its age. The air there is among the cleanest in the United States. The Colorado River running through the canyon continues to create more erosion. Widely considered to be one of the seven natural wonders of the world, the Grand Canyon lived up to its reputation.

"Let the heavens rejoice, and let the earth be glad; let the sea roar, and the fullness thereof. Let the field be joyful, and all that is therein: then shall all the trees of the wood rejoice."

Psalm 96:11-12

"There was somewhere, if you knew where to find it, some place where money could be made like drawing water from a well, some Big Rock Candy Mountain where life was effortless and rich and unrestricted and full of adventure and action, where something could be had for nothing."
From the novel
The Big Rock Candy Mountain by Wallace Stegner

Utah – named after the Native American tribe 'Ute' which means 'people of the mountains'.

May 2021

We visited and hiked in the stunning Bryce Canyon, drove to Zion National Park, and saw the majesty of Arches National Park. Utah, with mountains and deserts, deep canyons and towering red rocks, is a beautiful state. I love some of the Utah puns: "Utah's beauty is *rock* solid", "Utah *rocks*" and "This state is be-Utah-ful".

We chose a bicycle path to ride near Elsinore, Utah, and we could not have chosen a more scenic path. The Candy Mountain Express Bike Trail is a paved well-maintained trail in Sevier Canyon. We started at Sevier Junction South. The trail cuts through outcrops of volcanic tuff. On the way to Big Rock Candy Mountain, the pedaling is a mellow cruise. It follows an old railroad grade as it proceeds southward along the Sevier River through Sevier Canyon to Big Rock Candy Mountain. The uphill climb has only 250 feet of elevation change.

Robert and Evelyn Lee

After riding this awesome trail from Sevier Junction south and back (a roundtrip of 13.5 miles), we decided to continue the trail for a short distance although it extends another nine miles north and east to Elsinore. This section has short, steep grades and almost no shade, passing through farm country.

The Candy Mountain Express Bike Trail follows part of the route of the former Marysvale Line of the Denver and Rio Grande Western Railroad. Along its route are old mining and railroad sights. The Eagle Rock Railroad Tunnel, seen from the trail, was originally planned to be included in the Bike Path. It was not feasible due to the cost and the loss of historic value in order to retrofit the tunnel to safe standards. This tunnel, completed in 1896, measures 200 feet in length. It is curved to accommodate the Sevier River. There is an historic marker along the trail, and you can see through the tunnel near this marker.

There is a country folk song about a hobo's idea of paradise which was popular in 1939, hitting #1 on the country music charts. This version was cleaned up a little from the version in the 1890's, when the song described a child being recruited into hobo life by tales of the "big rock candy mountain". The song *Big Rock Candy Mountain* achieved more widespread popularity in 1949 when a new sanitized version intended for children was re-recorded by Burl Ives. In this popular version, "cigarette trees" become peppermint trees, and the "streams of alcohol" trickling down the rocks become streams of lemonade. The lake of gin is not mentioned, and the lake of whiskey becomes a lake of soda pop. What was once a horror story warning the dangers of the hobo lifestyle is now a beloved kids' song of a child's dream about a magical land of lemonade streams and candy.

Beyond the Handlebars Part 2

Big Rock Candy Mountain at Marysvale, Utah, was named after the song. The mountain is a combination of sulphur, alunite and other colorful minerals. It looks like it is covered with rock candy, with striped rose colored hills.

If you are ever in Utah and you drive down scenic highway 89, be sure to check out the Big Rock Candy Mountain in the Sevier River Canyon.

"In the Big Rock Candy Mountains,
There's a land that's fair and bright....
Where the sun shines every day....
Oh, the buzzin' of the bees in the peppermint trees
'Round the soda water fountains
And the lemonade springs and the bluebird sings
In the Big Rock Candy Mountains."

"You came down also upon Mount Sinai, and spoke with them from heaven, and gave them right ordinances and true laws, good statutes and commandments."
    Nehemiah 9:13   New Revised Standard Version

Robert and Evelyn Lee

"Keep your face to the sunshine, and you cannot see the shadow. It's what sunflowers do."
Helen Keller

Kansas – The Sunflower State

May 2021

    The Arkansas (pronounced Ar-Kansas) River Bike Path is Wichita's longest and most popular bicycle trail. The trail runs through a number of beautiful parks. While riding this trail through Wichita, you can visit some of Wichita's top sites. The Exploration Place, a science education center, is on the west side of the Arkansas River. This center, according to the brochures and advertisements, "inspires a deeper understanding of science and technology through creative and fun experiences for all". Unfortunately, it was closed the day we rode the trail. Other museums nearby include: The Wichita Art Museum, Old Cowtown Museum (re-creation of late 1800's Wichita), Museum of World Treasures, and the Mid-American All-Indian Museum.

    As you ride this trail south to north, you won't miss the Keeper of the Plains to your right. This 44-foot sculpture stands at the confluence of the Big and Little Arkansas rivers with hands raised to the Great Spirit. A tribute to the Native American tribes and donated to the citizens of Wichita by renowned Native American artist Blackbear Bosin, the Keeper of the Plains is surrounded by a plaza which describes the Plains Indian way of life. Dedicated in 1974 with Senator Bob Dole on hand, the area is free and open to the public. People gather near the Keeper during its nightly Ring of Fire ceremony, watching as five fire drums illuminate the statue and the water below. After the fire drums are lit, they burn for 15 minutes to symbolize the completion of the sacred hoop of the four elements of earth, air, water and fire.

We enjoyed our ride on the Arkansas River Bike Path in Wichita, Kansas.

"Then spoke Jesus again unto them, saying, I am the light of the world: he that followeth me shall not walk in darkness, but shall have the light of life."

John 8:12

Beyond the Handlebars Part 2

"I do not wish any reward but to know I have done the right thing."
Quote from the *Adventures of Huckleberry Finn*

New York — Elmira, New York, was the place that Mark Twain penned many of his finest works.

July 2021

As we were driving toward Elmira, New York, to ride the Lackawanna Trail, I was reading about the area of Corning, Horseheads, and Elmira. We learned Elmira was the summer home of writer Mark Twain, and he was buried there. We decided to take a few minutes to stop at Woodlawn Cemetery and see the final resting place of one of America's finest writers, Samuel Langhorne Clemens. Writing under the pen name Mark Twain, Clemens gave us some memorable characters — among them Tom Sawyer and Huckleberry Finn. Samuel Clemens' wife and children are buried there in the family plot as well. Olivia Langdon, Samuel's wife, was from Elmira. Halley's Comet appeared in the sky when Mark Twain was born in 1835. He died in 1910, just as the comet made its next pass within sight of earth.

It is clear Mark Twain loved to write. From his writings, it appears he had a skepticism about religion. He believed in God, he attended church, and he donated money for the construction of a church. But his personal faith and his experiences led him to skewer religious hypocrisy wherever he found it. He considered his best work to be "Joan of Arc", a reverential biographical account of a Catholic saint who exhibited all the human ideals Twain found so lacking in the rest of mankind. King Solomon also loved to write. Inspired by God, he wrote most of the book of Proverbs, writing in the first chapter that "the fear of the Lord is the beginning of knowledge". And in Ecclesiastes, Solomon penned inspirational words for those who write.

Before arriving in Elmira, we passed through Horseheads. During the American Revolutionary War, General George Washington ordered General John Sullivan to mount a raid on the Iroquois up the Susquehanna River. They went through what is now Horseheads to the Finger Lake Region and west to Geneseo. After devastating the Iroquois, the troops retreated back along the same route. By this time some of the horses were sick and disabled and had to be disposed of. The native Iroquois collected the skulls and arranged them in a line along the trail. The Iroquois named this spot "valley of the horses' heads". This is how Horseheads, New York, got its name.

The Lackawanna Rail Trail connects Lowman, New York, with Elmira along the Chemung River, a tributary of the Susquehanna River. The trail was very well maintained and an easy ride. On one side the river was visible for most of the ride with the other side being I-86. The trail was screened from the expressway with big woods most of the way.

After riding the trail, we stopped at the Corning outlet store, which has for sale Corningware, Pyrex, and Corelle, among other newer brands which make up the company Instant Brands. We had eaten the night before in Corning's Gaffer District. Mooney's had great food. The atmosphere was Irish Pub mixed with Sports Bar. They had a very large menu. Mooney's has been recognized as one of the top places in the nation to get great Mac 'n Cheese. Corning's Town Square was one of the most beautiful town squares we have seen. The Corning Museum of Glass has remarkable creations of glass art and artifacts. The Rockwell Museum in Corning, a Smithsonian affiliate, features a collection of Native American Art and other exhibits of "Art About America".

"And moreover, because the preacher was wise, he still taught the people knowledge; yea, he gave good heed, and sought out, and set in order many proverbs. The preacher sought to find out acceptable words: and that which was written was upright, even words of truth. The words of the wise are as goads and as nails fastened by the masters of assemblies, which are given from one shepherd."
Ecclesiastes 12:9-11

"Be like the cliff against which the waves continually break; but it stands firm and tames the fury of the water around it."

Marcus Aurelius

Connecticut – The Hartford Courant, founded in 1764, is the oldest continuously published newspaper in the United States.

Rhode Island – smallest state in size in the United States

September 2021

The Farmington River Trail is located in central Connecticut, approximately twelve miles west of Hartford. The Trail passes through the towns of Farmington, Unionville, Collinsville, and Canton. A portion of the trail has some points where users can stop and take in the breathtaking views of the river. One such portion of exceptional beauty was between Unionville and Collinsville. After riding this trail, we headed for Rhode Island where we had more adventures.

One of the most popular Newport, Rhode Island attractions is 40 steps and The Cliff Walk. The Walk is a three and one-half mile National Recreation Trail where one can view the beauty of Narragansett Bay. The 40 steps are a popular stopping point along this trail. These steps used to be a hangout for the servants of the wealthy owners of the Newport mansions during the Gilded Age. The servants, in their little free time, came to the steps to dance, listen to music and take in the breathtakingly beautiful views of the Bay. The Breakers is the grandest of Newport's mansions and a symbol of the Vanderbilt family's social and financial preeminence in turn-of-the-century America. The Breakers was completed in 1895. It is now open daily for self-guided tours. Since we started out early in the day to walk The Cliff Walk and the 40 steps, we still had the afternoon to ride a bicycle trail in Rhode Island. We had to park about one and one-half miles from The Cliff Walk, so by the time we were ready to leave Newport around noon, we had walked between five and six miles, taking in gorgeous views of the Bay and the very busy city of Newport.

The trail we chose to bicycle in Rhode Island, the Washington Secondary Bike Trail, was well maintained and had some very picturesque areas. The difference here from other states in which we have bicycled was the walkers walked toward the bicyclists, as would be on roads. Normally, walkers proceed on the right going the same direction as bicyclists on the trails. But in Rhode Island the rule is ride on the right, walkers walk on the left facing oncoming bicyclists.

Sections of the trail have their own distinct local names – Cranston Bike Path, Warwick Bike Path, West Warwick Greenway, Coventry Greenway, and Trestle Trail. The transition to each section is seamless. The trail is part of the developing East Coast Greenway to connect paths throughout New England and all the way down to Florida.

Beyond the Handlebars Part 2

"He is the Rock, his works are perfect, and all his ways are just. A faithful God who does no wrong, upright and just is he."
    Deuteronomy 32:4   New International Version

"I only went out for a walk and finally concluded to stay out till sundown, for going out, I found, was really going in."
John Muir

Massachusetts – Landing place of the Mayflower and the Pilgrims.

September 2021

    We wanted to visit an island while in New England, and since the ferry ride to Martha's Vineyard was just 55 minutes, we chose Martha's Vineyard. We chose the ferry that went to Oak Bluffs because one can pick up a bicycle path from there to Edgartown – a seven-mile bicycle trail. Oak Bluffs has a collection of Victorian gingerbread cottages built by the island's Methodist community. On our ride back from Edgartown to Oak Bluffs, we rode past these charming candy-colored cottages.

    The ride to Edgartown was pleasant, with the Nantucket Sound on one side and the 7-acre Sengekontacket Pond on the other. The trail is mostly flat. It is very popular because of the stunning views.

    While in Edgartown, we had time for lunch and chose a place with outdoor seating – Among the Flowers. Among the Flowers was a lovely breakfast and lunch venue. I chose breakfast and Bob had lunch – both were very delicious. It was a delightful experience. Edgartown is an elegant community. Walking down its streets, bordered by charming white cottages with porch and rose gardens, was enjoyable.

Beyond the Handlebars Part 2

Seeing the lovely shops, restaurants and art galleries added to the experience.

The following day while still in Massachusetts, we rode the Bruce Freeman Rail Trail – a trail from Lowell/Chelmsford to Acton. The trail was paved, wide, well-maintained and mostly flat. It has good tree cover for the majority of the ride. Bruce Freeman was a Massachusetts state representative from 1969 to 1986 and championed the creation of the trail. It is continually being extended. The nearly 24 miles roundtrip between Lowell and Acton was enjoyable on a beautiful day in September.

"Go Outdoors 2021" was a campaign in the area where people were encouraged to share works of art that transform various types of recycled doors into celebratory and intriguing works of art. The doors were originally placed along the Bruce Freeman Rail Trail in the summer of 2020 and were so popular it continued to spread to more communities in the area in 2021. "Go Outdoors – Neighbors" has continued to spread with new art doors installed or planned in seven additional cities and eight villages in the region. The public art project identified the artist and name of their design alongside the installed finished works of art.

The mission of "Go Outdoors" was to show the people in these communities what they might discover if, on foot or wheel, they found themselves on a path through the woods. Would they find a sensory world awaits if they leave electronics behind? Would they discover inspiration, whimsy, joy, reflection or spirituality?

"Finally, brethren, whatsoever things are true, whatsoever things are honest, whatsoever things are just, whatsoever things are pure, whatsoever things are lovely, whatsoever

Robert and Evelyn Lee

things are of good report; if there be any virtue, and if there be any praise, think on these things."

Philippians 4:8

"A house built on granite and strong foundations, not even the onslaught of pouring rain, gushing torrents and strong winds will be able to pull down."

Haile Selassie

Maine — the Pine Tree state, is the northeasternmost state in the United States and the only state with a one-syllable name

New Hampshire — The Granite State

September 2021

The Kennebec River Rail Trail in Maine is a paved trail following along the Kennebec River and offers many scenic views of the water and surrounding areas. We began our ride at the south end of the trail in Gardiner, traversing through the towns of Farmingdale and Hallowell, to the trail's end in the capital city of Augusta. On our way back, we noticed the many small shops and eateries in the town of Hallowell, perfect timing to get a bite and rest a bit before entering the more remote part of the trail following the river all the way into Gardiner.

New Hampshire has extensive granite formations and quarries. It also has quaint small towns among its beautiful landscapes. There are also large expenses of wilderness. We visited this state and drove through the White Mountain

National Forest. In the White Mountains are moose, black bears and part of the Appalachian Trail. We hoped to see the black bears and a moose, but it was not to be. We did see parts of the Appalachian Trail and marveled at how far north the trail came. And it goes up into Maine, so we were not even at the northern part of it. The Trail is a 2,180 plus mile public footpath managed by the National Park Service, United States Forest Service, Appalachian Trail Conservancy, numerous state agencies and thousands of volunteers. The Trail runs from Georgia to Maine.

In the southern part of New Hampshire, we enjoyed bicycling two trails – The Windham Rail Trail and the Derry Rail Trail. The towns are adjacent and the trails connected. Windham is one of the fastest growing towns not only in New Hampshire but in New England as a whole. Derry is larger (the fourth most populous community in New Hampshire), and it is known as "Spacetown". Derry is the birthplace of Alan Shepard, the first astronaut from the United States in space. The poet Robert Frost made his home in Derry for a time. Derry was first settled by Scots-Irish families in 1719 and named after the city of Derry in Ireland. The first potato planted in the United States was sown in Derry in the town's common field in 1719.

The two connected trails were a delight. They were both very well maintained and went through woodsy areas and a few marshy areas where sounds of nature prevail. The trails follow a railbed taken out of service by the Boston and Maine Railroad in 1980. A three-mile section through Windham cost the most to build because of extensive rock cutting. The trails are highly rated and we agree with these reviews.

Beyond the Handlebars Part 2

"Whosoever cometh to me, and heareth my sayings, and doeth them, I will show you to whom he is like: He is like a man which built a house, and digged deep, and laid the foundation on a rock: and when the flood arose, the stream beat vehemently upon that house, and could not shake it: for it was founded upon a rock." Luke 6:47-48

"When through the woods and forest glades I wander, And hear the birds sing sweetly in the trees; When I look down from lofty mountain grandeur, And hear the brook and feel the gentle breeze".
From the hymn *How Great Thou Art*

Vermont – The Green Mountain State – home of maple syrup

September 2021

We rode our bicycles in Burlington, Vermont, on the South Burlington Recreation Path and on the Island Line Rail Trail including the Burlington Greenway. Part of our ride took us along Lake Champlain as we rolled through waterfront parks. The Burlington Greenway was newly paved and had been beautifully landscaped. Beginning our ride at Overlook Park, we were treated with spectacular views of Lake Champlain and the mountains across the lake in New York. The ride on this South Burlington Recreation Path began with a heavily forested oasis of green, winding through more parks, tennis courts and playgrounds for children. While our ride this day was a bit difficult because of some hills and some heavy traffic at some of the crossings, we enjoyed this scenic ride and this beautiful city.

Church Street Marketplace in Burlington is a delightful space to stroll on a fall day in Vermont. The Marketplace was extremely busy on this Friday late afternoon, and we found parking places completely filled. Church Street Marketplace is a pedestrian street that has many stores; some chain stores and other local purveyors. There are some restaurants there as well. One of the original Ben & Jerry ice cream shops is at the Marketplace, as is David's Tea, Urban Outfitters, Patagonia Burlington, Lululemon, L L Bean, and many more. The street was filled with people. From what we heard, it is busy every day.

Visiting the Calvin Coolidge homestead in Plymouth Notch would take us through the Green Mountain National Forest area. This was a beautiful drive on a fall day. Leaves were near peak fall color. The homestead preserves many of the historic buildings that Coolidge knew in his youth: his birthplace, his boyhood home, the church that he attended, and the hall above his father's old store, which he used as his office during the summers of his Presidency. Seven generations of Coolidges are buried in the town cemetery, including Calvin and his popular wife Grace. Since Calvin was very shy as a child and a reluctant conversationalist as an adult, Grace was an asset to him. When President Harding died in August, 1923, Vice President Calvin Coolidge became the 30th President of the United States. Coolidge's actions and his reputation for personal honesty restored public confidence in the government. He encouraged prosecution of those involved in the scandals of the Harding administration. He won reelection in 1924 and despite his increasing popularity, chose not to run for reelection in 1928. He had been a traditional conservative Republican in his domestic policy, and opposed Federal programs that he saw as threats to individual freedom and initiative. He also opposed most international agreements.

Before heading home, we decided to take a tour boat to Heart Island, on the St. Lawrence River. There we toured Boldt Castle, built by George Boldt, millionaire proprietor of the Waldorf Astoria Hotel in New York City. Building the castle as a display of love for his wife, he began having 300 workers start in 1900, but when his beloved wife suddenly died in 1904, he stopped the project and never went back to the island. Seventy-three years later, in 1977, the Castle was purchased and since has been restored and improved for visitors in future generations.

We also visited Burrville Cider Mill in Watertown, NY, and we thoroughly enjoyed this tour. They, of course, had donuts, cider and fresh apples for sale. The pretty waterfall there made for a nice photo opportunity.

"Then shall the trees of the wood sing out at the presence of the Lord, because he cometh to judge the earth. O give thanks unto the Lord; for he is good; for his mercy endureth for ever."

1 Chronicles 16:33-34

Beyond the Handlebars Part 2

Robert and Evelyn Lee

"Winter is an etching, spring a watercolor, summer an oil painting and autumn a mosaic of them all."
Stanley Horowitz

Pennsylvania — Jim Thorpe, the first Native American to win a gold medal for the United States in the Olympics, is buried in Pennsylvania.

October 2021

On a fall day in late October, we drove to Jim Thorpe, Pennsylvania. The purpose was to ride the Lehigh Gorge Trail on a day when fall colors were at their peak. The foliage did not disappoint. The Pocono Mountain Shuttle Service, for a fee, drove us and our bicycles north 25 miles to White Haven. There we embarked on a 25-mile bicycle ride along the Lehigh River back to Jim Thorpe. There had been a heavy rain the day before, so there were no whitewater rafting trips this day. Along our way, there were waterfalls on our right and the river on the left. There was plenty of white water rushing. The drop in elevation on the 25-mile trip was approximately 600 feet. The trail was hard pack crushed limestone. The drop in elevation made the ride enjoyable. While still having to pedal the entire route, it was a rather easy ride, and the fall colors made it all the more enjoyable. The sound of water rushing was evident, sometimes so loud we had trouble hearing our own conversations.

After finishing our ride, we visited the Jim Thorpe gravesite and memorial park. We learned why this borough (previously named Mauch Chunk, being Place of the Bear in Native American language) was renamed for the first Native American to win a gold medal for the United States in the Olympics.

Oklahoma, Thorpe's birthplace, failed to erect a memorial for him. Thorpe's third wife took Thorpe's body and had it shipped to Pennsylvania when she heard that the small towns of Mauch Chunk and East Mauch Chunk were seeking to attract business. The towns "bought" Thorpe's remains, erected a monument to him, merged, and renamed the new borough in his honor as Jim Thorpe, Pennsylvania. He had never been there. However, he had attended the Carlisle Indian Industrial School in Carlisle, Pennsylvania, in his younger years.

Jim Thorpe was considered one of the most versatile athletes of modern sports. He won two Olympic gold medals in the 1912 Summer Olympics (pentathlon and decathlon). "Sir, you are the greatest athlete in the World" – King Gustave of Sweden at the 1912 Olympics. Thorpe also played collegiate and professional football, professional baseball, and basketball. Later in his career, between 1921 and 1923, he helped organize and played for the Oorang Indians (LaRue, Ohio), an all-Native American NFL team. The team was organized to promote the sale of Airedale dogs, by Walter Lingo, a local businessman and entrepreneur. Between 1926 and 1928, Jim Thorpe played for the "World Famous Indians" of LaRue, a traveling basketball team. We note this LaRue, Ohio, connection since Bob was raised near LaRue and heard many stories about Thorpe during his growing up years.

The borough of Jim Thorpe, Pennsylvania, was a very busy place. The Mauch Chunk Museum and Cultural Center details the area's coal mining history, and the life of the town's namesake, Jim Thorpe. The Lehigh Gorge Scenic

Beyond the Handlebars Part 2

Railway takes passengers into Lehigh Gorge State Park. Whitewater rafting and bicycling adventures abound in this historic area of the Pocono Mountains.

"Daniel answered and said, Blessed be the name of the Lord for ever and ever; for wisdom and might are his: And he changeth the times and the seasons; he removeth kings, and setteth up kings: he giveth wisdom unto the wise, and knowledge to them that know understanding."
Daniel 2:20-21

Robert and Evelyn Lee

"The duty of the branch is to cling to the vine."
Max Lucado

Virginia — Mount Rogers, elevation 5729 feet, is the highest point in Virginia.

November 2021

Virginia creeper, or five-leaved ivy, is a species of flowering vine in the grape family. It is a prolific deciduous climber, reaching heights of 70-100 feet in the wild. Vigorous and fast growing, Virginia creeper provides a nearly carefree addition to the landscape, producing one of the most spectacular color displays of fall. The five-pointed leaves, usually green, turn a brilliant crimson once temperatures cool.

Naturally, we assumed the Virginia Creeper Trail got its name from the vine known as Virginia creeper. We rode this wonderful trail in November while fall color was still brilliant and learned the nickname "Virginia Creeper" came from the early steam locomotives as they slowly struggled up the mountains. However, the moniker was also a nod to the vine prevalent in the region.

The trail is approximately 35 miles and connects Abingdon, Virginia, with the Virginia-North Carolina border, 1.1 miles east of Whitetop Station, Virginia. The trail began as a Native American towpath. Later, it was used by European pioneers including Daniel Boone. By the early 1900's, the Virginia-Carolina Railroad ran from Abingdon, Virginia, to

Elkland, North Carolina, hauling lumber, iron ore, supplies and passengers. Failing to show a profit since before the Great Depression, the Creeper ran its last train on March 31, 1977.

Upon arriving in Abingdon, we took the shuttle to Whitetop Station, through the Mount Rogers National Recreation Area, a portion of which the trail runs through. The first 17 miles riding from Whitetop Station to Damascus descends from 3576 feet elevation to 1952 feet. No cell phone service exists on this 17-mile section of the trail. The surface of the trail is cinder, crushed limestone and dirt. There are many rocks and some washed out rutted areas, especially on the first three miles. The surface is better as you get further along.

There are 47 trestles along the route, all numbered at either end of the bridge. The length of these trestles are anywhere from 100 feet to more than 600 feet. On the trail, you will cross the Appalachian Trail. By the time you get to Damascus, you will have crossed 30 trestle bridges. Here, at Damascus, the Appalachian Trail runs down Main Street.

The second part of the trail, from Damascus to Abingdon, is wider and more flat and winds through rolling farmland. The elevation goes from 1952 feet at Damascus to 2087 feet at Abingdon. The remaining 17 trestles are on this section, which is also very scenic.

The Virginia Creeper Trail is beautiful. The views are incredible. Lots of river and forest views and some farmland views make for a very pleasant experience. We rode on our hybrid bicycles and, while most riders had mountain bikes, we did fine. We would not recommend road bicycles. There are some ruts and rocky areas that jar your head a little. All in all, we enjoyed this nearly 35 miles very much.

Beyond the Handlebars Part 2

"I am the true vine, and my Father is the husbandman. Every branch in me that beareth not fruit he taketh away: and every branch that beareth fruit, he purgeth it, that it may bring forth more fruit. Now ye are clean through the word which I have spoken unto you.

Abide in me, and I in you. As the branch cannot bear fruit of itself, except it abide in the vine; no more can ye, except ye abide in me. I am the vine, ye are the branches: he that abideth in me, and I in him, the same bringeth forth much fruit: for without me ye can do nothing."

John 15:1-5

"In a small town, everyone works together and does life together, and because of that everyone takes care of each other. That's Iowa. Whether it's Des Moines or Sioux Center, Decorah or Davenport, Iowans exhibit those small-town values. They work hard, but not so much for themselves. They're ambitious, but not at the expense of others."

Kim Reynolds

Iowa — Every year thousands of people bike across the state, west to east, as part of the RAGBRAI Celebration (Register's Annual Great Bicycle Ride Across Iowa), a celebration of Iowa's small towns and community culture.

December 2021

We drove to Iowa to bicycle the High Trestle Trail near Des Moines. The capital of Iowa was moved to Des Moines in 1857, having previously been Iowa City. Des Moines, as the state's capital, is the site of the first presidential caucuses of the presidential primaries.

Des Moines is home to many insurance companies, thus earning the nickname "Hartford of the West". Headquartered there are Principal Financial Group, Fidelity and Guaranty Life, Wellmark Blue Cross Blue Shield and others.

Beyond the Handlebars Part 2

We decided we wanted to see the Iowa State Capitol, being it is one of two capitols to feature five domes, a central golden dome surrounded by four small domes. The other is the Rhode Island State House. A favorite of visitors, the Iowa State Capitol Building features a 275-foot, 23-karat gold leaved dome in the center flanked by the four smaller domes. It is a beautiful building. As it was nearly closing time, we drove by and stopped to take photos but did not arrive in time for a tour of the interior, which we understand is ornate and features a grand staircase, a five-story law library and a collection of first lady dolls.

The High Trestle Trail, a 25-mile concrete and asphalt trail, includes a one-half mile, 13-story high bridge across the Des Moines River Valley. The trail runs along the Union Pacific Railroad's discontinued stretch of train line between Woodward and Ankeny. The trestle bridge, "From Here to There", is one of the most well-known rail-trail art installations in the country. With a nod to the area's coal-mining history, traveling the bridge feels like going down a mine shaft with its 43 twisting diamond-shaped steel ribs lined with LED lights. There is a timeline that starts with a period 13,000 years ago and continues to the present. All along the timeline, it shows various events that occurred during the passage of time. It makes one think that you are just a "blip" in time on the way to the next 13,000 years, and beyond. After dark, the bridge comes alive as blue lights illuminate the steel cribbings.

The trail proceeds through Iowa farmland and some forested areas, then over small creeks and open lands. The trail is very well maintained and fairly flat, making for an easy and very enjoyable ride.

While we were in Iowa, we drove through small towns and thought of the movie, "Field of Dreams", about an Iowa farmer who built a baseball field on his land after hearing a voice saying "if you build it, he will come". Former baseball greats start emerging from the fields to play ball. And later, the farmer's deceased father shows up as one of the players. The farmer had been estranged from his father and never patched things up while his father was living. The movie ends with them playing pitch and catch. He had realized his father probably had dreams but had never pursued them.

"Therefore, since we are surrounded by such a great cloud of witnesses, let us throw off everything that hinders and the sin that so easily entangles. And let us run with perseverance the race marked out for us, fixing our eyes on Jesus, the pioneer and perfecter of faith. For the joy set before him he endured the cross, scorning its shame, and sat down at the right hand of the throne of God. Consider him who endured such opposition from sinners, so that you will not grow weary and lose heart."

    Hebrews 12:1-3 New International Version
:

Beyond the Handlebars Part 2

> "We were lucky enough to grow up in an environment where there was always much encouragement to children to pursue intellectual interests; to investigate whatever aroused curiosity."
>
> Orville Wright

North Carolina – The Wright Brothers completed their first flight on the Outer Banks just south of Kitty Hawk, in a town now named Kill Devil Hills.

May 2022

We enjoyed reading the following quote from Wilbur Wright, the elder brother of the American aviation pioneers: "If I were giving a young man advice as to how he might succeed in life, I would say to him, pick out a good father and mother, and begin life in Ohio." Being from Ohio, we would have to agree with this sentiment.

While on the Outer Banks, we rode our bicycles, climbed to the top of the Currituck Beach Lighthouse, visited Kill Devil Hills and the Wright Brothers Memorial, went to the beach, and saw the Cape Hatteras Lighthouse.

The Currituck Beach Lighthouse, located in Corolla, has 220 steps to the top. It was a lovely view from the top. We rode our bicycles on the Corolla Greenway for much of the way from our lodging. There were a few miles on the road, but the majority of the 23-mile roundtrip was on the paved trails.

Beyond the Handlebars Part 2

The Cape Hatteras Lighthouse, with its black and white candy cane stripes, is one of the most famous and recognizable lighthouses in the world. It is the tallest brick lighthouse in the United States and, unfortunately, was closed to climbing the day we visited. The Cape Hatteras Lighthouse protects one of the most dangerous sections of the Atlantic Coast. Here, the Gulf Stream collides with the Virginia Drift, a current from Canada. Many, many shipwrecks here have given it the reputation of Graveyard of the Atlantic. Originally built in 1803 and extended with a brick addition in 1854, by 1862 extensive repairs were needed, and it was determined to be less expensive to build a new lighthouse. This was completed in 1870. Due to erosion at its base, the lighthouse was moved 1500 feet back from the ocean in 1999.

The Wright Brothers National Memorial in Kill Devil Hills was very well done. We rode our bicycles around this park several times. It was a very pleasant experience visiting the various monuments and displays commemorating the first airplane flight. The Wright Brothers certainly were focused on their interest in flying. Their dedication reminds me of the song by Hillsong United "Oceans (Where Feet May Fail)", based on Matthew 14:25-33. The song is about stepping into the unknown and keeping faith, trusting God, so that you can, "keep your eyes above the waves".

We enjoyed bicycling on the Outer Banks. The paved path along Route 12 in Avon gives bicyclists safety so that they don't have to ride on the busy Route 12. We enjoyed seeing the small towns along the way. The Corolla Greenway was a very pleasant ride.

And we really enjoyed bicycling around the park at Wright Brothers National Memorial near Kitty Hawk.

Robert and Evelyn Lee

"But they that wait upon the Lord shall renew their strength; they shall mount up with wings as eagles; they shall run, and not be weary; and they shall walk, and not faint."

Isaiah 40:31

Beyond the Handlebars Part 2

"In matters of principle, stand like a rock."
Thomas Jefferson

Indiana — The State's song is "On the Banks of the Wabash".

Ohio — Annie Oakley was born near Greenville, Ohio, and spent her entire childhood in the Buckeye State.

August 2022

We decided to take a short trip to Indiana to bicycle some trails. Our first stop was Wabash. The Wabash River Trail, newly built and dedicated with a ribbon-cutting ceremony in May 2022, was a delight. Running seven miles between Wabash and Lagro, the trail has small ups and downs as well as many curves which made it interesting as it paralleled the river. There were very few road crossings and, of course, being new the pavement was very smooth. In Wabash, the Wabash River Trail connects to the Wabash Riverwalk Trail, extending our ride to 16.5 miles round trip.

After finishing our ride, we visited Hanging Rock National Natural Landmark on the banks of the Wabash River near Lagro. Hanging Rock is approximately 420 million years old and was formed in the Silurian Period when much of the Midwest was covered by a shallow sea. The limestone reef deposits rise 75 feet above the River, and the top was left overhanging its base when the river undercut the rock.

We remained in Indiana the following day and enjoyed riding the Whitewater Gorge Trail and a portion of the Cardinal Greenway, both in Richmond. The Whitewater Gorge Trail, a small trail, connects to the much larger Cardinal Greenway, which runs 62 miles from Richmond to Marion. We have bicycled various parts of this trail in prior outings. We enjoyed this day and these well-maintained trails, stopping briefly at a very nice Veterans Park (the Wayne County Veterans Memorial Park) along the Whitewater Gorge Trail.

Before heading home, we stopped in Greenville, Ohio, to ride the Tecumseh Trail Multi-use Pathway. The trail is nearly 15 miles with about half on the paved dedicated trails and the other half share the road. We road various sections, both on road and on the trail, enjoying the Darke County countryside. In downtown Greenville, we stopped at the Annie Oakley Memorial Plaza, where sits a larger-than-life bronze statue of the small Wild West sharpshooter – who was born in Darke County near Brock, Ohio. Annie Oakley was not her real name as she was born Phoebe Ann Moses. Her family called her Annie and she chose Oakley as her professional surname after the name of an Ohio town near her home.

Chief Sitting Bull, the Sioux leader who orchestrated the defeat of General Custer's troops at the Battle of Little Bighorn, attended one of Oakley's Wild West show performances in St. Paul, Minnesota, in 1884. He was mesmerized by her marksmanship and dubbed her "Little Sure Shot".

We left Greenville and drove home via Route 36, enjoying a ride across Ohio passing through many small towns on our way back to Mount Vernon. A very pleasant stop at The Farmer's Daughter in Urbana, a country-style café with a down-home atmosphere, delicious food and good service, provided a nice break and much-needed energy for the remainder of the drive. It had been a very busy three days.

"Behold, I will stand before thee there upon the rock in Horeb; and thou shalt smite the rock, and there shall come water out of it, that the people may drink. And Moses did so in the sight of the elders of Israel."
Exodus 17:6

Denali is the third tallest of "the Seven Summits" (the tallest peak on each continent), after Mount Everest in Asia and Mount Aconcaqua in South America. Denali is actually the tallest mountain on land – even taller than Everest – if you measure it from the base to the summit.

Alaska – Ketchikan has the world's largest collection of totem poles.

September 2022

Ketchikan, Alaska, was one of our favorite stops on our cruise. It is where we rented bicycles and achieved our goal of bicycling in Alaska. We were excited to discover a protected bicycle path along the waterways just past the Coast Guard Base along the South Tongass Highway. The paved path followed the shoreline and provided excellent views of the Pacific Ocean waterways south of Ketchikan. We passed the Village of Saxman (famous for its Totems), Rotary Beach (popular community beach) and Mountain Point (south end of the trail and an excellent shore fishing spot).

Ketchikan was our last port prior to ending our 10-day cruisetour (three days on land and seven days on the cruise ship). The land portion was fabulous as we spent three days in Denali National Park. The scenery was spectacular. Starting in Fairbanks, we visited the Aurora Ice Museum in Chena Hot Springs Resort. The ice carvings were magnificent. We also put on our bathing suits and ventured into the Chena Hot Springs. The natural hot springs turned out to be hotter than expected but very relaxing with beautiful surroundings.

Robert and Evelyn Lee

The heat from the Earth's interior can indeed by very hot. The tour guides gave us each a bottle of cold water which we appreciated – you do feel a bit dehydrated after being in the springs.

The next few days included a train ride through Denali National Park, bus rides to hotels, a stop in Talkeetna (a turn of the 20th century gold mining center and launch point for climbing expeditions to Denali). Mount Denali (formerly Mount McKinley) is visible from Talkeetna with gorgeous views of the mountain if the weather cooperates. While a little cloudy the day we were there, we did get to see the mountain from our lodging. We also experienced a day with some rainfall for at least a part of the day. Soon the snow would begin falling, as it can begin in September in Denali National Park. Also, while aboard one of the buses, we saw a moose; although we were a little slow in turning our heads so saw only about 80% of the moose as it rounded a corner.

We boarded our cruise ship in Whittier, near Anchorage, and spent seven wonderful days at sea, with stops in Skagway, Juneau, and Ketchikan. In Skagway, we took the White Pass and Yukon Route Railway, with fantastic scenery and beautiful waterfalls in abundance. The Mendenhall Glacier near Juneau was a great side trip as well. We were able to get a close-up photo of this glacier with its dazzling blue colors.

While on board the ship, we had plenty of activities in which to participate. The naturalist gave talks which were very interesting, the music entertainment was very good, and the trivia games were fun. We saw lots of humpback whales, usually in groups of about five or six, having fun in the waters not far from our ship.

A highlight on board the ship was a special dinner. Our children honored Bob with a surprise chocolate cake and celebration of it being the 50th state he has visited, completing a goal of visiting all 50 states. Holly and John Taylor, the friends we traveled with, helped with this surprise. Holly and John are our son's in-laws.

Exhausted after the cruise, but very happy to have seen Alaska and bicycled there, we ended our cruise in Vancouver, British Columbia.

"For as the rain comes down, and the snow from heaven, and do not return there, but water the earth, and make it bring forth and bud, that it may give seed to the sower and bread to the eater, so shall My word be that goes forth from My mouth; it shall not return to Me void, but it shall accomplish what I please, and it shall prosper in the thing for which I sent it."

Isaiah 55:10-11

Robert and Evelyn Lee

"The man is blessed who every day is permitted to behold anything so pure and serene as the western sky at sunset, while revolutions vex the world."
                                            Henry David Thoreau

Idaho – The main producer of potatoes in the United States.

Washington – The evergreen state. Forests cover over half the state.

September 2022

Because of a flight delay, we were forced to find a spot where we could rent bicycles and ride in Idaho and Washington the same day. How lucky we were to find Coeur d'Alene, Idaho. Bicycle rentals were abundant there, and they had a wonderful paved trail (Centennial Trail) which was 62 miles with 23 of them in Idaho continuing nearly 40 miles in the state of Washington to Spokane. We were attempting to ride in all 50 states and since we were in this area, we wanted to make sure we rode in Idaho, Washington and Oregon. Now left with just two days to ride before our flight home, and while we did not ride the entire trail, we achieved the goal of riding these two states. The following day, we would ride in Oregon.

The Centennial Trail was well maintained. The weather was perfect, and we were blessed with much beautiful scenery. Lake Coeur d'Alene was spectacular. While there, we hiked Tubbs Hill. Tubbs Hill Park and Nature Trail is bordered by Lake Coeur d'Alene. Tubbs Hill is 120 acres with a 2.4 mile hiking trail. Along this trail are amazing views of the Lake. There are several spots along the trail to sit in awe of the scenery. Beaches and swimming areas can be found on this hike as well.

When you reach the State of Washington by bicycle on the Centennial Trail, the trail name becomes the Spokane River Centennial State Park Trail. The trail traverses through high desert Ponderosa pine forests, basalt canyons, hip urban centers and cultural heritage sites. More than 40 significant historical sites dot this trail, among which are the 1974 World's Fair Site, the Great Northern Railroad depot clock tower built in 1902, and Slaughter Camp Monument where 800 Indian horses were killed to discourage future uprisings. We did not get to see all of these, but were grateful to the bicycle rental place that delivered bicycles to where we wanted to start riding and had us lock them and take a picture of where we left them so they could pick them up at their convenience. The business name was Cheap and Easy Bikes, owned by a 15 year old boy, who couldn't even drive, yet. Mom was helping out. Entrepreneurship at its best!

As we left this area, making our way to Oregon, we were impressed with the beautiful sunsets. It's hard not to think of the divine when witnessing such gorgeous skies.

"Far and wide they'll come to a stop, they'll stare in awe, in wonder. Dawn and dusk take turns calling, 'Come and worship'."

Psalm 65:8 The Message Bible

"It's a wonderful feeling to be a bridge to the past and unite generations."
— Vin Scully

Oregon – Nicknamed the Beaver State. The state animal is the American Beaver and the reverse side of the state flag depicts a beaver.

September 2022

The Banks-Vernonia Trail, the first "rails to trails" path in Oregon, was a delight. The 21-mile trail features 13 bridges. The views from the 733-foot long, 80-foot high Buxton Trestle were spectacular.

We needed to rent bicycles and were pleased to find a bicycle rental store right next to the trail. The owners also ran a dance studio next door to the bike shop. The owners were very helpful. They measured us to make sure we got the best bicycles to be comfortable as we rode. They made sure we took helmets out of the freezer, as they proclaimed freezing makes sure the helmets were sanitized properly.

The Banks-Vernonia Trail was paved, well-maintained, fairly wide, and followed an abandoned railroad bed between the cities of Banks and Vernonia. There was a slight uphill from Banks for several miles. The slight downhill came as you approached Vernonia, the north end of the trail.

Robert and Evelyn Lee

We were extremely thankful we were able to ride this Oregon Trail as our flight out of Seattle was scheduled for the following morning.

"Blessed are the peacemakers: for they shall be called the children of God."

Matthew 5:9

"Take a walk down a dusty Lowcountry road on a warm summer evening. Sit on a swing and watch the tide come in. Stand with your feet in the salty ocean water. Close your eyes and smell the pluff mud. And then you'll know my heart."

Elizabeth Bishop Later, ouryardfarmhome.com

North Carolina – has three distinct regions: The Appalachian Mountains covers the western region, the Piedmont Region is a plateau that sits between the mountains and the Coastal Plain region in the eastern part of the state, which leads to the Atlantic Ocean.

South Carolina – The Lowcountry is defined as the Southern, Easternmost area of the Palmetto State.

January 2023

During the cold winter days of late January in Ohio, we decided to take a trip to the Carolinas to ride some trails. Upon arriving at our first stop in Gilkey, North Carolina, the weather being a pleasant 55 degrees, we set forth on the Thermal Belt Rail-Trail. The wide well-maintained trail is 13.5 miles long, ending in Forest City, North Carolina. What an absolute gem! The trail appeared to be recently paved – a very smooth ride running through quaint towns. The charming small towns of Spindale, Rutherfordton and Ruth were pleasant to ride through. A highlight of the ride is its passage by the Bechtler Mint Site Historic Park, where gold was mined and gold coins were minted in the mid-1800s.

Overall, the 27-mile roundtrip is a great ride if you find yourself in this area of North Carolina.

Our second stop – after a good night's sleep – was the Doodle Trail, which runs from Easley to Pickens, South Carolina. This trail in the northwestern corner of the state, was opened in 2015, is 8.5 miles long, neatly paved and well maintained. The railway which began in 1898 was called the "Doodle" because it ran backwards like a doodlebug between Pickens and Easley due to its inability to turn around. The Doodle Trail had absolutely gorgeous scenery. The seventeen mile roundtrip ride gave us a good cardio workout as there are some challenging hills, which also led to some sweet slopes to glide down. Most of the hills were long and gradual, making it doable without having to get off and walk the bicycles. We rode from Easley to Pickens and back. Pickens is tucked in the foothills of the Blue Ridge Mountains. The natural beauty of the mountainous surroundings is evident there. As you enter Pickens on the trail, a beautiful mural, "where the mountains begin", awaits for your viewing. Bob's bicycle chain was rubbing, making it a more difficult ride for him, so after our ride we went to Papa Wheelie's, a bicycle repair shop in Easley. He fixed us right up, assuring Bob his next ride would be more smooth.

Beyond the Handlebars Part 2

Another restful night and we were off to Beaufort, South Carolina, to ride the Spanish Moss Trail. By now, the temperature would reach the low 70s. Construction of the Spanish Moss Trail began in 2012 and will eventually cover 16 scenic miles through Beaufort County between Port Royal and Yamassee. When we rode here, a total of 10 miles had been completed. This concrete trail was very flat, a wide trail with beautiful scenic marsh areas. This Lowcountry trail was busy with friendly locals out for walks. Dolphins are occasionally seen here, but on this day we didn't see any. Beaufort is located on Port Royal Island, one of the largest Sea Islands along the southeast Atlantic coast. It is known for its antebellum mansions, especially in the downtown historic district. Located in the heart of the Sea Islands and South Carolina Lowcountry, the city is also known for its military establishment, being located in close proximity to Parris Island and a U S naval hospital, in addition to being home of the Marine Corps Air Station Beaufort.

"Oh, that you had listened to my commands! Then you would have had peace flowing like a gentle river and righteousness rolling over you like waves in the sea."
       Isaiah 48:18 New Living Translation

"Moses spent 40 years thinking he was somebody, 40 years learning he was nobody, and 40 discovering what God can do with a nobody."

D. L. Moody

Pennsylvania – Lancaster was the capital of the United States for one day – when the Continental Congress met there in 1777.

August 2023

We traveled to Lancaster, PA, Sight and Sound Theatre to attend the performance of "Moses". We enjoyed this show in a packed house. The theatre, which seats 2,000, featured a 300 foot panoramic stage that wrapped around the audience on three sides. While Moses is best known for things like the burning bush, the plagues and the parting of the Red Sea, we learned that Moses was a relatable man who struggled with being able to speak succinctly. He needed help with his journey to find himself – with an identity and destiny found solely in God.

The following day, we decided to bicycle the Northwest Lancaster River Trail. This trail was paved and well maintained and is just over 14 miles in length. And there were so many things to see. The White Cliffs of Conoy was a unique landmark which formed over time by the waste products of a limestone quarry. This created a very hilly area of limestone cliffs on the shores of the Susquehanna. Most of the trail follows along the Susquehanna River. Near the

Beyond the Handlebars Part 2

southeast end of the trail, rock climbers can be seen scaling the craggy face of Chickies Rock. There is also a tunnel to ride through – the Chickies Rock Tunnel. This tunnel, said to be haunted, is only 180 feet long and was blasted through solid rock in the 1850's when it was built for the Pennsylvania Railroad.

We highly recommend the Northwest Lancaster River Trail. You will ride through wooded areas, farmland, and along the amazing scenery of the Susquehanna River with side paths to the river.

And while in the Lancaster area, take in a show at the Sight and Sound Theatre.

"Come now therefore, and I will send thee unto Pharaoh, that thou mayest bring forth my people the children of Israel out of Egypt. And Moses said unto God, Behold, when I come unto the children of Israel, and shall say unto them, the God of your fathers hath sent me unto you; and they shall say to me, What is his name? what shall I say unto them? And God said unto Moses, I AM THAT I AM: and he said, Thus shalt thou say unto the children of Israel, I AM hath sent me unto you."

Exodus 3: 10,13,14

> "Agriculture is our wisest pursuit, because it will in the end contribute most to real wealth, good morals and happiness."
>
> Thomas Jefferson

Nevada — Lake Tahoe, straddling both Nevada and California, is the largest freshwater lake in the Sierra Nevada and the largest alpine lake in North America.

California — Over a third of the country's vegetables and nearly three-quarters of the country's fruits and nuts are grown in California.

September 2023

The trails we rode in Nevada were nicely paved and well maintained. The Erica Grief Trail in Sparks parallels Veteran's Parkway, which connects Sparks to Reno. The trail was named for a University of Nevada, Reno student and cycling enthusiast who died in 2015 in a car accident on her way to a California bike race. It is said that Erica, known as the Reno Rocket, would ride even in the snow. She put zip ties around her wheels for traction, and off she'd go.

Beyond the Handlebars Part 2

The trail we rode in South Lake Tahoe, the Stateline-to-Stateline Trail, is only partly complete. When finished, it will run entirely in Nevada along the eastern shore of Lake Tahoe and connect at the California State Line on both the south and north end of the trail.

South Lake Tahoe was a beautiful area. Visiting in September turned out to be a good choice. There were fewer crowds, while still very warm weather. While riding along the eastern shore, we realized there's a reason Lake Tahoe ranks as one of the most beautiful lakes in the United States. The stunningly brilliant turquoise colored water, which heretofore we'd only seen in pictures, was visible for much of the bicycle ride.

On our way toward Bakersfield, CA, we drove through Yosemite National Park. We spent three hours in the Park, mostly in the car enjoying the wonderful scenery, stopping occasionally at photo opportunities. We enjoyed seeing the giant sequoia trees, Bridalveil Fall, and the granite cliffs of El Capitan and Half Dome.

In California, we rode the Kern River Parkway Trail in Bakersfield. This trail was nicely paved and very well maintained. It is an easy and flat ride. We parked in the parking area for the trail across the street from Cal State. Riding west from there to the western end and back was approximately 23 miles. About a mile into the ride, there was a 5K race (3.1 miles) to benefit cancer research. With what appeared to be several thousand walkers and runners on the trail, we walked our bicycles until the racers turned around at the halfway point to head back to the sign at the 3.1 mile finish line. It was nice to see so many people supporting this cause. As we kept riding west, we left the urban environment for a very rural one, entering an area known as the "Bakersfield 2800". It is 2800 acres of watershed/flood control. No water, no toilets, no food for about 10 miles. They have a signed gate that gives you fair warning about this area. You will be in the middle of nowhere. Be on the lookout for rattlesnakes, coyotes, foxes, rabbits, roadrunners and red tailed hawks. The trail ends on Enos Lane, still in the middle of nowhere. We rode back from there having seen several of these critters (rabbits, a hawk, a roadrunner and a snake).

While driving from Nevada to Bakersfield the preceding day, we saw miles and miles of nut and fruit trees. Kern County is among the top agriculture producing counties in the nation. In 2016, the county ranked number one in agriculture production. Migrant workers comprise a substantial portion of the population. A large portion of Kern County population is Hispanic. The people participating in the 5K race were mainly Hispanic.

We enjoyed the bicycle riding we did in both Nevada and California.

"The sluggard will not plow by reason of the cold; Therefore shall he beg in harvest, and have nothing."

Proverbs 20:4

Beyond the Handlebars Part 2

"Because there's nothing more beautiful than the way the ocean refuses to stop kissing the shoreline, no matter how many times it's sent away."

Sarah Kay

Kauai – Hawaii's fourth largest island is nicknamed "The Garden Isle" thanks to the tropical rainforest covering much of its surface.

September 2023

In Kauai, Hawaii, we had reserved rental bicycles at Hele on Kauai Bike Rentals. This rental place was just seven miles from Lihue Airport, so we took a taxi after learning it would be three hours to get the rental car we had reserved. Seems the rental company couldn't find employees or decided to staff only one employee that particular day. As it turned out, taking the taxi and canceling the car rental worked out just great.

The Ke Ala Hele Makalae bicycle path in Kapa'a starts at Lyngate State Park and follows the coast north ending at Ahihi Point. The paved, well maintained path is awash with magnificent scenery, gentle breezes, and lots of photo opportunities.

Ke Ala Hele Makalae (the Path that Goes by the Coast) runs along almost eight miles of the east side of Kauai. All along the trail, interpretive signs share information about local archeological, cultural and historic sites. For over four miles, riding along the Pacific Ocean, one is treated to the stunning vistas along Kauai's picturesque shoreline. Breathtaking coastal cliffs, golden sand beaches, and lush vegetation line the route.

On the drive between the airport and Kapa'a, we stopped at the 'Opaeka'a Falls area and lookout. The awe-inspiring view of 'Opaeka'a Falls, with its breathtaking beauty, features a 151-foot waterfall and a lush, tropical ravine. The dense vegetation surrounding the waterfall has vibrant shades of green, which provide a stark contrast to the white veil of water. The lookout provides a safe vantage point to view the scenery.

Another falls near Kapa'a is the Ho'opi'i Falls. These falls were used in the filming of Jurassic Park. This one has a rather difficult trail and is in a residential neighborhood. While researching this trail, we learned some sections had extreme mud and sketchy areas down steep slopes. There is very little parking available and some reviews said people get lost. But the cliff at the falls, which is 20 feet high, is one of the most popular cliff jumping spots in Kauai. You should only jump if you are with a local who knows exactly which spots are safe for taking the plunge. This area also has a second falls in an even more primitive part and becomes a dense rainforest feel. Some reviews even said it was illegal and just for use by the neighborhood kids. We didn't visit this falls but noted the interesting articles about this area.

The west side of Kauai features Waimea Canyon, described as "The Grand Canyon of the Pacific". The Canyon is 14 miles long, one mile wide, and more than 3,600 feet deep. The Lookout there provides panoramic views. There are numerous trails for both beginners and seasoned hikers.

One thing very noticeable on the island was the feral chickens. These wild chickens outnumber the residents by six to one, and there are various theories as to where they came from. Most locals say the first wave came ashore with the Polynesians over 1,000 years ago. The chickens were very colorful, especially the roosters. They sported brilliant ruby-toned hackles, tall combs and shiny multi-color coats. It appeared to us these hens and roosters had an air of entitlement. And it turns out there is a state law which prohibits harming them in any way. But it also seems most folks there enjoy the presence of their beautiful birds. They are not eaten, as the meat is tough, and their eggs are not good, either. The roosters cock-a-doodle-do all day. Sometimes noisily. In short, Kauai is no place to be chicken of the chickens.

Kauai is a beautiful island. As it turned out, our 50-state bicycle riding goal was completed there in the 50th state. We had a picture taken while holding a "Congrats on 50 States" placard.

"That Christ may dwell in your hearts by faith; that ye, being rooted and grounded by love, May be able to comprehend with all saints what is the breadth, and length, and depth, and height; and to know the love of Christ, which passeth knowledge, that ye might be filled with all the fullness of God."

Ephesians 3:17-19

www.ingramcontent.com/pod-product-compliance
Lightning Source LLC
Chambersburg PA
CBHW070241090526
44586CB00035B/1372